Frank Zappa
& Barry Manilow

ISBN-13: 978-0692639078

Morgan Drolet
and
Shawn Sullivan

NEON BURRITO PUBLISHING

▲ 1 △

Morgan Christopher Drolet

Born in California. Long Walks.

Shawn Michael Sullivan

Grew up in a Bellbrook Ohio television.

I

A mumbling drunk walks by the plaza
Taps the wall twice without stopping
Mumbles on
Standing under Sunset shadow sidewalk sunglasses
She
Drove here from Saskatchewan
Land of living skies
She grew from that place of untamed
A smooth quartz action frame death party with a
wink

II

It's dark early now
Sitting
In the basement of the Hotel Alexandria members of
the staff
Because it's Christmas
Are wrapping the leaks on swollen pipes with rags
rope and duct tape
Or in the ballroom placing pots and pie tins to catch
dripping plaster
Hastily brainstorming treatment for the melting wall
paper
Up
Stairs
A young girl allows herself to seep hollow into
swimming night
The lobby war games play out to a score by Dylan
An a haggard scrap miner makes a local bet on the
horses
From a panhandle phone in roman alcove burning

III

i'm so sorry trumpets are playing
they're noisy
and

i can't ask them to stop
i mean i did ask them to stop
they said i can't ask that from them

IV

his backpack is on his back
his skateboard is on his backpack
his helmet is golden and sparkly
his jacket is royal blue and fits tight
his motorcycle turns left
his street is fairfax to beverly
don't stop that smile

V

Thin faced ol black man on a bike
blue neon wheels flash past
Glitter dripping from Santa hats on mannequin Melrose
Where he slangs the sleigh caps on the go
Burning rubber to a halt he repositions his gear
Almost clobbered by a Chrysler
He shakes his head
watching West Hollywood elementary's student of the
month drive off
An idler in a black mustache pins a pink shadow on a
crippled staircase
With two jackets on
I watch the laughing bare thighs breathing little sex
sighs
Shimmy down the cloistered blvd
As if preening albatross
A steam propelled hangover cloud spurts from waxing philosophical moon
A young drunk upends his guts on the bus
'I guess I drank a little too much'
He spits
All the legs with all their shoes hover
Above the leaking slosh of puke
There's a dog eared ole scamp trying t pawn a hot
pocket watch for a cold drink
And he maneuvers like a grape on a clean white plate

VI

Those days
When we boiled over with careless oblivion
Before the parties had metal utensils and glass cups
When everything was plastic or straight from the bot-
tle
In parks or wooded areas
We'd light things on fire and pluck guitars
We still hated hippies then
In those militant over nothing days
And when you left at night
Us with our dirt still burning
Trophies of empty bottles built in corners
Where did you find us again
Out on the roads
On reds
With cases full of clothes
Where pawned guitars once have idled
Or up about houses
Dry and swaggering on the bluffs
We cast rocks and shadows and demons into the sea
We took jobs as fishermen
Trailing long lines into the heaving green darkness
Sleeping on the sand
With salt spray alarm clocks
Rising with freedom limbs waving
Brushing off centuries old erosion
Or we left you searching
Some under the ground
Others with new masks
Unrecognizable

VII

He always trimmed his nails on the stoop where he
could watch the city breathe
Fritos magazine subscriptions palm fronds
Overflow the trashcan seeping each morning at the
corner
Diamond eyed storefronts wink and shuffle wide
A pregnant riot gurl waddles past in bouncing soles
Her "does your pussy riot?" shirt painted on like eye-
liner
Past Tikum the schizophrenic mute who carries on
his monologues in sign language
He feigns left
BAM!
And he's off like an injured horse

VIII

oops
terrible plan
i'm being honest
everything's pungentish

my soul is the assistant manager
my souls wants to quit
says "enough! beetles
scurry in your heart"

my soul won't stomp my bugs
the bugs won't escape
the bugs will kill my soul
i'm sure my soul will die

no matter what anyone does
there'll be my sadness

IX

"suspicion often creates what it suspects."
c.s. lewis

"oh fuck. is that true? goddamnit. i did it again."
~barry manilow

everyone who will be in this room
is already in this room
the room is paradisiacal,
almost

except
everyone hates me right now

i said the wrong thing
the shift occurred
between me being a guest
and me being an intruder

well there i think i went
so there i go

catastrophes
destroy lives you know
i feel catastrophes because of catastrophe
some feel like it
but they're different
i can't explain

X

when other-dimensional guests visit
to learn about humans
i won't be a distinguished detail

skip me and fully understand humans anyway
i'm an example of an existence
not the greatest, not the chosen

but, you know
when i go missing, important or not
some of the spectrum goes missing

i'm the kind all twisted and reckless and
wild, whenever possible
that's me and that's the kind i like

you get up to your business
let's chat later
i'm being crazy

XI

one night, a hang thing
zero attendees knew how to start a party
but there was a party

they knew what we were up to
there were stories to drink and listen
madness blossomed
insanity was present
people crumbled
no one minded

like, barry
who treasures sci-fi,
physics, logic, video games,
larping, horror movies,
black metal, net sins,
and terrific breakfast deals
he's with the group
he has his bottle of whiskey
and talks about his vacation to denmark

anthony, gold chained and alive
sits beside emily as long as he can, like two minutes
he drifts away, emily still plays the piano
drew tickles emily's shoulders once, twice
he wonders if emily likes his new jacket
sally stands drinking beer and watching
emily play the piano
emily plays the piano to play the piano
they drink her when they can
they drink when and what they can when they can

none of this is doctor recommended
none of this is good advice
these people are full of malfunctions
they're mapping into destruction
true
but, tell you what
if they have what they create
and what they create is tragic
at least they are having and creating

he snorts coke with thomas in the bedroom
they share things with each other they didn't know
they'd share
the drug does its thing as long as it does
they feel better
they feel worse
they know they feel
they agree they can't count on present moments
moments betray them and they betray moments
they don't know for sure what to feel
they know there is somehow a group thing around
them
wonderful

XII

Two eyes murmur in their wicks
Almost blank with high frequency penetration
The stars seem like loosed olive pits falling
Shouting as they do in voices thick with sweet table
wines and mahogany perfume
Let em fly man
We got our own trip to plan
High stoic shadows of well postured men seemed
stretched
High and thin
from a distance
Planted in spring loaded bucket seats
Bolted above rows of slashing gears in dreaming
They wield the mouths of thrashers trundling over
half golden eaves in hysteria
Keep left at the fork
Keep from under the knife
Keepon ki pinnon
Somewhere traffic keeps time within its I.v. Dripdrip
drip......
And this faucet agrees

XIII

all of us
all 7 billion of us
let's gather together

well, nevermind
that's difficult

hmm, is it possible to
form a global circle
or a kinda humungous box vortex

a crazy shape thing
wow

embarrassing
embarrassing suggestions
ok,

ok, ok. if it's not probable, there's
the party:

walk away at the beginning
for heidegger moments
if those call you

phone people might sit down
and feel comfortable
while eating
with legs curled under their bodies
alone, except not by themselves
persons making make believe

like adolfo bioy casares
a bummer, their fancy dinners
there're such low guest counts
not everyone's invited

persons both imaginative and serious
sad and beautiful
like fernando pessoa
are loved
they can't love back
and they're loved

someone hunts a bear in the front yard
the person doesn't chat much
the pool is full of people
kayaks float down the river

i got a real problem
who's going to eat snacks with me?
nobody!

the snack table doesn't even like me
i'm more like
probably outside smoking a cigarette (of course)
with one person i didn't choose

though you gotta realize
this is also pretend
invite whomever
tiger woods for example
i'm pretending

you can't stop me
you're not invited
you're trying to be invited
you're not invited

(p.s.
crash the party if you want to,
duh)

XIV

Listening to bill collectors ring I
Step out into tolling streets of Spanish Harlem
Just before pavement pops to broiling
With the little white mutt Chanto
Who's loved by the clack nailed PR women with their
breasts like rockets that frighten braziers and the seam
straining thighs
"ay Chanto! Como esta papi?"
The men on stoops gleaming or shaded bronze
Draped in generations down staircases
She told me to have him back quick
To the loft where cigarette fed plants wheeze on the
fire escape
But we're rolling now
Me an this lively mutt
Who stops to sit at a souvenir shop
Pouty lipped pr girl cast of pure sex at 13 feeds Chan-
to a pickle
Slipping her hands across her curves she smiles from
shadow eyes and my heart aches at her artistry
Turning left there's still relics of the old days
The dirty days not sure but true
And the baroque faced mutt leads the way
Back
To the loft with the plants and the girl
Who wants to hang furs in her closet and dance up-
town

XV

people looking at pyramids see
impressive giant tombs

you don't have to explain

i'm talking about big big egyptian pyramids
although other pyramids exist
tiny egyptian pyramids
mesoamerican pyramids
the great pyramid of cholula

(
btw,
mayans:
notable artistic success
in 2012
)

anyway
i don't think one needs to read essays
to like pyramids
you don't need to know quetzalcoatl
or khafra or menkaure or khufu themselves
you can check out their pyramids

cultural foundations
scientific principles
architectural achievements
topics like that
for the essays, the books, the history
i like to see things

that's what i most cherish
i haven't seen the pyramids

this wasn't written while i was in a pyramid
sadly
although
anyone could read this while in a pyramid
recommended

of course what i want is to kiss lee by a pyramid
or just to cuddle with lee while we cruise the gaza
strip in a car

XVI

this isn't a party
oh, this is a party
i'm partly me, you're partly you
we're standing on the balcony
revolving people actions pass by us
i'm pinching my cigarette
you're tapping the banister
you drink your beer you slug your booze
your face turns red you sweat
you tell me everything wrong and meaningless
so i adore you
we know we're meant to be on this balcony
it's the place for us
because we have nowhere else to go
we both know the secret
we visited to talk with others
knowing we had no one to talk with
nothing to say
we know about our blues
we don't really talk about them
we have cigarettes to pinch
booze to sneak inside
we kiss the terrible, as much as we can

terrible things
we adore you
you'll stay terrible for others
we adore you
trying our best here
we're trying our best

XVII

together with you on a random afternoon
i noticed we noticed everything terrible about me

when with you the next day
you and i wanted to be free and uncaged and we for-
got everything

the day after that we feel uncertain

a week later it was like i never saw you
i felt awful and that was my fault

i woke up and felt wonderful
because i have to want to

then i woke up and felt terrible
because i'm meant to

later, we ate pizza and mentioned things
i'd been reading gombrowicz's ferdydurke
you'd been reading bolaño's savage detectives
we related to each other's cultural adventures
our minds shared new thoughts

how do these thoughts enter our lives
how does the read become the happening

are we strong enough to do this?
scary question

we wondered and we hoped and what is tomorrow

the world wasn't what we wanted
are we what the world wanted?
we didn't know
the world didn't know
so we agreed
we must keep going anyway
we know we must
we know nothing else except we must keep going
we must keep living
our pizza was tasty

the next day i wrote a poem and said
the world is as bad as it can be or
i'm as scared as i can be
yes, it's the last that's me for sure

i want to funnel myself into culture
find a community
happy to be alive -- alive --- at least

art culture is self-help for the soul
andbut there are so many self-help books
so many with the same theme, of bettering oneselves
everyone can't all be reading the same ones

there are so many different types
the figurative and the literal
the dying on the inside the dying on the outside

i have a real problem
about converting my philosophy into life
converting my thoughts into more than feelings

what i know is
i'm magnetized to those with broken fences
those whose whole front yards have the folk of the
wild
cougars and sloths

wolves and chickens
bears and cats
animals chilling so nice and electric and free
they can be rowdy

i'll know what i can
i'll be rowdy
i'll be so rowdy it'll be like i didn't learn anything
i'll be so free i won't teach anyone anything

since i can't die when i want to
since i can't know when i'll die
i'll live when i want to

you'll always be right
those who are right
you'll never win me
those who want to win me
i got shit to do

XVIII

I skate by on rubber soles
On grey white pools of rippling sidewalk
The red terra cotta tiles seem to slumber bright and
rumbling
The umbrella faces pass at clipped stride on hurried
feet
Girls boots up to the knee
Thud smack! Thud smack!
With scarf colored around their necks dangle swank
and loose or sharp and utilitarian
Me liking it as an insight
Lines of people rake the city blocks for sales
4 dead 75 wounded last count
2 men define mortality in a shoot out at toys r us
The rain swings north
Leaving a trim blanket of chill clear sinking blue

XIX

When the girls dance in the streets
Feet fighting on simmering concrete
Where will you be
When the summoners and thieves are shackled to
their words
(A tin lip squiggled below a nose wriggles)
Will you be in Bradford or New Orleans when the sky
calm and stately blue
Is slowly bundled in canvas flags that mumble causti-
cally jubilant
How resplendent natives weave yesterday masks for
you dreaming
How will you receive them
If in this dream you have no face
But a red russet potato where a face once dwelt
From your window does the moon dawdle
In its half naked glee as it did when
The moors ransacked the country home of dry creak-
ing ancestral dust
Do not tremble in the presents of the hoodoo man
His power
(And he say yours)
Comes from bone
Watch him play the sacred root
Will you wonder at the old way
The whisper days of blood majik
With your eastern eyes set westbound
Can you still bleed a crowd of laughter
In your new chameleon tombs

XX

little bugs scares me
ok, honestly
bugs scare me in general
i know the big ones will wallop me
what will the little ones do

XXI

i thought about the awful
you were there
how do you feel about that?
i think you should feel ok
to be included in my thoughts
just, don't become a nazi
you know
otherwise, it's cool
i'm trying too

XXII

Some stretched out fool on the orange 14 to Alvarado
He's got shoes off
16 crooked toes with three digits each
Throwing Cheetos round like money in a titty bar
And he's falling apart at the seams
Got the dropsies something fierce
This morning some cat on a bike creeps by panning
for change
He's streamlined the operation
The burger stand pinned up
Slowing out with greasy nocturnal nostalgia
The cops across from Linda's Place beer & wine
creep
As the white brick beams green neath or red street-
light
Hanging melodrama 'round the queer Latinos in rec-
onciliation post explosive betrayal
I've got a dull burn for tacos
And the teal eyes staring psychic wafts stale whimsy
from her sheets
Into the boulevard and west

XXIII

I watched a man the shape of a bleeding "s"
Crooked an wobbly from cystic fibrosis
Worn crutches with slippery feet to bolt on his fore-
arms each morning
His complexion a pleading bewilderment
Flashing in stuttering flame headlights
He attempts the long journey from the east bank of
fairfax to the west
drivers lunge at their horns
Their well working feet itching to punch the petals
It's Christmas for Christ sake
No time to waste on this cracked robot hobble
Who sits to rest on cold green bench

XXIV

for a period of time, it's always true --
without your words i am dead
i can't go on without you

at my best i can realize
when i stand crumbled before you
i made the decision
to see myself as crumbled

i treasure when you tell me i'm not crumbled
when you remind me of you as a person
when you remind me of me as a person

but if i'm right about not being crumbled
i shouldn't have to hear it
if i'm right
i'm right in the first place

i'll try to believe that
you can try to push me back to standing when
you want to
because, it's true
i keep going for you
of course
i hope it's obvious

XXV

Chanting ex pats of chemical seduction
Suck at trembling bone china near the limestone
crumble steps of a Chinese haberdashery
Drinking in coffee scented corridors the consistency
of faded sails
Someone's cracking knuckles like a whip
An the boys on the corner dig into deeper pocket
warmth reserves
Beating down the butts and copper and cellophane
crinkle
The grinding whir and smoke electric crowns of
commercial rigs
Jog down endless gasping 3rd st
A hook nosed skirt on the corner drips earrings and
baubles that refract raw molasses like
Wrapt in feathered tinsel
Shoulders oscillate greedily search out a hustle
Eyes painted in mirror match graffiti growth near her
kitchenette garden wall
2nd generation swoll lipped super leeches shedding
lizard breath as he drops into his finances
Grumbling his hand me down problems
Doling out broken promises for broken things to ten-
ants all breaking or broken
A pack of feral patchwork cats whine systematic for
the old wrinkle glazed woman
She feeds them unleavened bread and regales the alley
with her omens of skeletal winged serpents and woe

XXVI

A clean whistle cut and varied through the slices of
city blocks descending
Hey bainey! Gimme a cigarette. But bainey's hand
nods he's busy as he passes
I don't smoke those
That's a woman's brand anyhow
Down the corner stacks
of drums lookin ever like
Like liquor
Stills
Brown rust rings soak down the edge the age
They thud at night like elastic waistbands snapped
against flesh
There's a power line spitting raw electric fuzz
A rubber singe coffee hymn lingers
The kitchen light pops on yellowy at the donut shop
And this puke on the sidewalks gettin me paid to
clean it
Out here the blvd.
on its drop cloth of neon
Pants under the steel eyed stereo night

BLESS XX